VENUS RISING FROM THE SEA

A Collection of

Seascapes in Verse

Cover Art

Birth of Venus
detail of the centre, c.1485
(tempera on canvas)
By Sandro Botticelli (1444/5-1510)
Located in the Galleria degli Uffizi, Florence, Italy
De Agostini Picture Library / A. Dagli Orti
The Bridgeman Art Library

VENUS RISING FROM THE SEA

A Collection of

Seascapes in Verse

By

Patricia Anne Kirby Craddock

First Edition

Copyright © 2014

Pontifex Press, LLC
Atlanta, Georgia

Pontifex Press, LLC, Atlanta, GA

Published in 2014 by Pontifex Press, LLC.
Distributed to the trade by Lulu Press, Inc.

ISBN-10: 0-9913009-1-2
ISBN-13: 978-0-9913009-1-4

Visit Pontifex Press's website at www.PontifexPress.com

Book design and layout by Stephanie N. Bryan

Cover Art: *Birth of Venus*
detail of the centre, c.1485 (tempera on canvas)
By Sandro Botticelli (1444/5-1510)
Located in the Galleria degli Uffizi, Florence, Italy
Copyright © De Agostini Picture Library / A. Dagli Orti
The Bridgeman Art Library

Rear Cover image of a scalloped shell by Stephanie N. Bryan

Printed in the United States of America

ACKNOWLEDGMENTS

"At Sea in the Indian Ocean" was published in *Northwoods Journal,* Thomaston, Maine, Vol. XI, No. 1, Fall 2003.

"Love Duet" came out in The International Library of Poetry Anthology, *The Best Poems and Poets of 2005,* Owings Mill, Maryland, 2005.

"Neptune's Playground" was published in *The International Biographical Center Magazine*, Cambridge, England, Summer 1984.

"Point of View" appeared in *The International Biographical Center Magazine*, Cambridge, England, 1989.

"Portrait of a Peregrine Falcon" was published in *Art Times*, Mt. Marion, NY, July/August 2011.

"Sonnet To a Seagull" came out in *North American Mentor Magazine*, Fennimore, Wisconsin, 1973, and in NAMM's *Down to Earth Poems*, Fennimore, Wisconsin, 1976.

"St. Simon's Island, Georgia" was published in *O Georgia*, Humpus Bumpus Books, Cumming, Georgia 1996.

"Sunday Afternoon" appeared in *North American Mentor Magazine*, Fennimore, Wisconsin, 1974.

DEDICATION

To my grandson,

Andrew Stephen Kirby,

who is as restless in spirit and open to the elements,

and to new places and experiences,

as the sea itself.

"And God said, Let the waters under the heaven
be gathered together unto one place,
and let the dry land appear;
and it was so,
And God called the dry land Earth;
and the gathering together of the waters
called he Seas;
and God saw that it was good."

—The Bible (King James Version)
Genesis 1:9, 10

VENUS RISING FROM THE SEA

Table of Contents

THE SEA !   (A Preface)

What writer-poet can pay fitting tribute, in poetry or prose, to its timeless beauty, its eternal mysteries? What artist can portray on canvas its majesty and might—so humanly inconceivable, so divinely conceived and formed? What photographer can record on film its unfathomed depths and myriad life forms? Composers, too, endeavor to evoke *Il mare's* haunting melodies, the throbbing rhythms of *La Mer*. Poets may be the last to admit defeat in our common artistic passion to depict sea-shaped reality. But still we try, even though the oceans of the world are essentially unknowable, unconquerable by man—in ships, in words, in art. Gazing and venturing upon them in wonder we can only value them as they are: awe—and fear—inspiring and yet, soothing balm to our restless human spirit. We know, to the bottom of our being—deep as *their* deepest depths—that oceans are laws unto themselves: supreme examples of God's matchless Creation and of man's yearning, too, to create, to prove we are indeed made in His grand and glorious image.

And so we do ceaselessly endeavor to capture the sea's elusive essence in art, to answer its endless call, its irresistible pull of tempest and tide, to speak to it in kind. Inland-born and bred, I myself simply exist between pilgrimages to sea and shore. I'm ever eager to experience and explore them, even in imagination—as in this modest collection of poetic seascapes of some of the world's great waters, and the rare living creatures, great and small, still abounding therein: one poet's passion, deep and wide as the seas themselves, for God's unquenchable gifts to man. Like a child yet-to-be-born, feeling a mother's heart comfortingly beating against the confines of our first salty-sweet, liquid home, I become fully alive when near the sea, my own pulsing heart echoing those steadily pounding waves. So, mesmerized, I hold on to my poetic images—to measure them somehow in words, to hoard them for the future, against the inevitable time of going back to my prosaic earthbound world, against my longed-for return, yet again, to the sea.

THE SEA ! (continued)

As a southeasterner, I know well the shores of the Atlantic Ocean and the Gulf of Mexico, although I've never sailed upon them; and I have steamboat-cruised along the great Mississippi River. Every large body of water, including the River Rhine, exerts its own fascination. But there are oceans and seas, rivers and lakes I've never seen and probably never shall, except in imagination: the Pacific, Mediterranean, Adriatic...When I'm standing upon some never-too-desolate shore, however, they too are there, more real than real, those other distant, tempting beaches and seas. To support world efforts to safeguard for future generations our four great oceans—Atlantic, Pacific, Arctic and Indian—and all of their water denizens: whale and dolphin, shark and squid, sea lion and fish...and to perpetuate our appreciation—if only by immortalizing them in poetry— is my highest aim. What if, like all extinct bird and animal species, we had only memories of our oceans, our seas, and their inhabitants? If in experiencing these few poems, we writer and reader, can together feel and find ourselves somehow pleasurably, or dangerously, *there*—on some sun-lit or stormy shore—then I'll know that we share a worthy goal and dream, we lovers of the sea.

(Afterword)   Since beginning this imaginative seafaring odyssey-in-verse, I had the good fortune to go on a 35-day once-around-the-world/once-in-a-lifetime cruise with my late Navy veteran husband of six years, who long inspired me with *his* great love for the sea, and some of my dreamed-of oceans became reality! Some of these poems were composed on our long voyage by water and sea, Atlantic to Mediterranean, Indian to Pacific. I hope that they all may awaken in you my own love affair with the world's great oceans and seas—and the same longing to do all we can to preserve them—so you, too may be moved to create your own unique, ongoing homage, in word and deed, to God's *"gathering together of the waters."* *BON VOYAGE!*

—Patricia Anne Kirby Craddock

VENUS RISING FROM THE SEA

(after Botticelli's *Nascita di Venere*)

I step from my bath like Venus
emerging from the sea,
my ocean cascading rivulets
down all the valleys and hills,
the sunlight and shadows of me.
My hair wet, trailing
its wavy veils unbound,
I wait for such waves of love
to enwreathe me like the wind,
the only ethereal barrier reef
between thee and me. I set my feet
upon earth, eager in my quest already
hearing your voice your kisses sweet
floating on air: how lovely, how fair...

SEA BIRDS

SUNDAY AFTERNOON, December 7, 1941

(Sunshine Beach, St. Petersburg, Florida)

Tsunami-like, these waters have raced
over half a world to lap and taste
this temptingly vulnerable southern shore.
Dazzled, long drenched in the beauty of each,
as by their playful, graceful spray,
I am lordly, profligate, turning my back
to the changeless, inviolable sand and sea.

My hand, grown weary
with the tossing of bread
to subservient gulls
wheeling and flapping
flatteringly toward me
from miles down the beach,
teases the radio dial, today,
trying to tempt it to say something
newer, somewhat more exciting
than this ancient day's coming Good News,
or the far less promising news of the day.

"We interrupt this program",
(your thoughts, lives...
dreaming, desiring...)
the ethereal voice agonizes,
"to tell you we are at war..."

(continuing)

(begin stanza 4)

The unalterable word assaults my senses
crawls in my ear like the poison it is—
dispatcher of kings and subjects and princes.
But I cannot bring myself to hate
the destroyer of my kingship, my kingdom,
but, rather, mourn the death of those beaches
already, and destined to be, violated.
Even now, the approaching, encroaching tides
claim these proffered shores, voluptuously waiting.
I gather my remnants of hope of pretending
that nothing has changed, and turn back
to the comfort of unending sameness,
the false consolation of not-quite-yet-knowing,
the growing feeling of no place to hide.

Reproving, remote, the gulls move oceanward,
sensing somehow I have lost control
of my role of benevolent power, protection
over beaches and creatures here and abroad—
those private recesses, sun-spangled reaches
whose sacrosanct beauty already is being
cruelly, violently desecrated.

SONNET TO A SEAGULL

Now, lifting my hand to shield my sight
from shadows dark against the bold, bright winging
of your and your white brothers' rhythmic flight,
I pause anew to marvel at your bringing
Eternity, who heaves her gentle signs
within your wingèd arc. Impatiently she cries!
And from her Bosom's curve, cold tears are flinging.

Impoverished hope and sovereign dream both plight
unmitigated troth in sea and me,
each knowing well, by sunlight and by night,
immortal or immortalized, that we
are chained in Time's unraveled dark. One interlude:
my soul's delight—of your unvarnished solitude.
Ah, life-enchanted one...you lover of the sea!

SEA BIRDS OF ST. SIMONS

Northward at dusk the sea birds fly
(to spend the night on Sea Isle?!).
Hundreds in flights of a dozen or more
pursuing their natural bent
for centuries (an aeon or two?).
Only now, they fly over me.

Gulls, pelicans stream from shore
into the deepening sky.
Do they soar over other beaches and seas—
or wander in dreams, as do we
from known to far unknown
reaches of destiny?

How lovely to be so free!
To ride on the tides of the wind and the sea.
Do our souls, too, yearn to return
past earthly horizons,
to transcend fate,
to fly to the ends of ocean and sky?

At dawn the sea birds serenely
flapping unhurriedly
turn back from their distant mysteries
to those eternally here:
sun, sand, and sea.

FAREWELL TO TYBEE

They've come to bid us good-bye
from their realms of air and sea,
these lords of the deep and the high
currents of ocean and sky.

A dozen brown pelicans fly
in slow and measured ease
northward to Hilton Head,
while southward the dolphins dive—
leaping, playful, alive—
to their rendezvous off Sea Isle.

If only we could hold on forever
to such passing delight. But we too
must go our ordained way
till our day of promised return.

ODE TO THE BIRDS IN THE TREES OF HILTON HEAD

(Pinckney Island National Wildlife Refuge, Hilton Head, S.C.)

Enwreathed in these fair canopies of green-leaved limbs,
sovereign in your Eden-Isle's covenant with earth,
as kings their crowns you wear arboreal diadems
and feathered wings, like Leda's swan, of royal birth...

Embracing Arcadian colonnades of moss-laced trees,
you creatures of peace in Paradise, your birthright,
evoke classic images in living art, a pure Greek frieze
arrayed in the timeless stillness, marble, carved in white.

*

O Ibis and Egret, Heron and Stork—you feel my gaze
and yet my soft, far-off footfalls raise no alarm
in this your other-world, in these, your halcyon days
Sanctuary undefiled, safe from harm.

The sound of your distant calls enthralls beyond words—
a muted humming, throbbing, joining of voices mating,
bespeaking love for shoreline and sea, all to be heard,
And when will sundown's silence fall? I'm waiting

(continuing)

8

(begin stanza 5)

for you, shy/sly ones, beguiled by the moon to roam
and hunt and mate *(and will you, too, for art's sake,*
speak as love's poetic muse?) in your marshland home—
O Armadillo and Raccoon, Alligator and Snake

But if bird and beast and man can meet only by chance,
as in this late afternoon's commune, even now at rest,
can we not, still, see—in every flowering being and branch—
Life...created and evolved, ever-present, manifest?

*

One worldly poet, overcome—by earthly poetry!
Clinging to the end, to such a romantic view
of some Divine Presence ...in you, in me...
Promising to return, commending all "à Dieu".

PORTRAIT OF A PEREGRINE FALCON

Regally you stand, there upon your painted promontory,
barren rocky crag crowning your domain of mountain, sky and sea,
windswept aerie of royal birds of prey—falcon, eagle, hawk.
After the storm, before your next fierce-diving flight, you pause
against a brilliant backdrop of brooding clouds, gray, majestic,
awe-awakening, pierced by the breaking torchlight of the sun,
eyeing distant sailing ships, adrift, unmanned, unthreatening.

How apt your artist consecrated to re-enact your being!
Lavishing such harmony, such surety of belonging
to your natural world, affirming the Creator's eye
in all our earthly eminence and His divine preeminence—
at this moment in time when we, artists-poets, still strive,
burning but to live to see ourselves so immortalized
in both art and nature's pure embodiment.

2305 CLUB LAKES PARKWAY

This morning the lake, through our window view,
lies still but shimmering—only a slight
air current stirring its polished face:
its burnished green-gold glaze reflecting
the willows gracefully bending, trailing
over its watery, bordering heights.

On the opposite side a blue heron steps
delicately out on his fragile perch,
fallen tree branches rimming the lake.
From time to time he unfolds his wings;
yards-wide they seem for he is great,
master and lord of all he surveys.

Ducks and geese we have in abundance:
families sailing flotillas of five
arriving in from brakes unknown
to alight with a splash on their favorite berth;
or strutting along the paths surrounding,
proudly herding their fleet-footed flocks.

But a Great Blue Heron is rare in these parts.
From what distant shore to this inland haven?
Quo vadis, heron, wings unfurled...?
You breathe mystery, glamour, tropic, exotic,
on our wistful, earthbound, landlocked ways,
as we gaze through our window to your watery world.

SEA CREATURES

ST. SIMONS ISLAND, Georgia

The ocean curls round my feet

Like the surf the sands
advance and retreat,
elemental as I in my
grasping at immortality.

Dimly glimpsed through the sea-spray's mist,
dazzling, shimmering, glittering haze,
other exotic, foreign, golden shores
take my breath away.

In the distance, two frolicking
sun-kissed porpoises play,
escaping the net another day.

Alone on the wide horizoned beach
my eyes, mind try
to comprehend, take in
the enormity of creation.
I bend for a handful of water, sand,
life abundant, unmeasured therein.
How many myriad species keep
watch in the sea's endless deep?

A generous wave tosses me
a coveted chambered shell.
Such delight!—then I see
its owner clinging, treasured therein,
trusting, as in our human frailty,
the immensity of creation,
the gentleness of those given dominion,
the benevolence of the Creator.

(continuing)

My far-reaching arm returns
the peaceful domiciled creature
back to its natural home.
A little act of playing
God—touching even me.

The ocean swirls around me

Like my dreams it seems to go on forever
embracing the world, and me.
Confiding, sometimes, its secret rhymes,
its eloquent, elegant prose
and poetry from the sea.
Even when it takes
the very ground from our feet
in its constant, rhythmic throes

I WOULD LOVE TO LIVE ON THE COAST OF MAINE

Inland-bound I dream and long
to belong by an eloquent sea...
her poet-creatures welcoming me
in porpoise/seabird prose and song.
Sea-yearning poet!—it's plain
I would sing with them some day
(and Longfellow, and Millay)
odes to our ocean home...to Maine.

DOLPHIN   (somewhere at sea)

"Dolphin off the port bow!",
the captain's loudspeaker shrieks,
and eager, we crowd portside to see
the friendly sea creatures who till now
played hide-and-seek
near and far.

"There they are!" —
diving and smiling and leaping
high as our deck in midair.
You can almost hear them cry,
"The tourists are back—
put on a good show!"

How loath we are to see them go.
Sleek and shining as raw Thai silk.
One moment here, the next goodbye
as, all too soon, to our holiday.
We can only grasp you, Dolphin,
and hold on to this moment in time,
in picture and prose and rhyme.

NEPTUNE'S PLAYGROUND

Flipper to flipper, side by side,
you roam the great horizons dividing
ocean from sky, sailing from flying.

Frolicking in your temperate waters,
soaring together, mated, unbound,
you surface with breathtaking sound and ease.

Who has painted you, sleek and shining—
grays and whites and seafoam green—
re-creating primordial beauty?

Who but your Artist's hand and eye
renders immortal your leap and dive,
tenderly forms you joyful, alive?

Sail on, O Dolphins—innocent, free.
Live on in your moment of effortless triumph.
Neptune is guarding your playground, the seas.

(From a painting of dolphins by Italian artist Athos
Menaboni, of Atlanta, Georgia and Livorno, Italy,
private collection)

VIEW FROM THE PACIFIC RIM

On the coast of British Columbia's Vancouver Island,
on the shore of Pacific Rim's National Park,
designer winter storms rage. Storms creating their own
gran spettacolo of wind and wave, of gale and whale.
Heedless spectators flock to the edges of precipices
on Wild Pacific Trail overlooking the sea,
standing in awe of Neptune, Poseidon and more
modern gods who, too, fling their salt-spumed might before
those who stand watch from their own more romantic view.

Two hundred fifty wrecked ships, lost during 200 years past, here lie
forever beneath the cold waves, in this vast Graveyard of the Pacific.

At certain times of the year tourists, onlookers seeking thrills
are rewarded by a glorious sight: pods of surfacing whales
from the 22,000 majestic gray whales migrating northward,
returning from their own *vaccances*—not in the South of France
on fashionable *côte d'azur!*—but in the sheltering embrace
of their familiar spawning grounds in the warm Sea of Cortes.
There, nestled between Mexico and California's Baja,
they frolic and mate and give birth before the urge to navigate,
to swim the five thousand miles back to answer the call to feed
in nature's cold, welcoming, plankton-rich, Bering and Chukchi seas.

JONAH AND THE WHALE

O Jonah daring turn away
from God's commending voice and glance...

What then?—if He has not allowed
for Ninevah a second chance
that ancient city, foolish, proud.
And for you.

You who hide your face from Him
sailing anywhere instead
of relaying His rebuke,
thinking to confound the Lord.
Now His sea-tossed tempest speaks
to warn you of His will.

But those unbounded winds and waves
bow to his saving grace to prove,
and moved to pity by your cry
from that resounding drowning place
He plucks you from eternal sleep
beneath those dark unfathomed deeps.

Then once more He rescues you
as His great commissioned fish
casts you on some timely shore
to bear at last His reprimand
before too late for Ninevah
to turn back from her worldly ways,
or else beget retribution:
the setting of her noonday sun.

(continuing)

Three days three nights you've rested here
God's gift of time to repent...
Yet when the Assyrian king and court
at your behest bedeck themselves
in sackcloth and in ashes, you,
lost in mockery and ire,
dare lament God's compassion
for Israel's enemy.

Better for you to so adorn
yourself, O vengeful Jonah, blessed
that His boundless mercy keeps
remorseful worlds like Ninevah
saint and sinner seeking finding
His pardon, His forgiveness.

THE FLOOD

When in the beginning a mighty wind
swept over the depths of the abyss
the primordial oceans the salt water seas
the Lord created His great sea monsters
all swimming beings even before
those on land, and man. O Lord, was thy heart
so soon aggrieved by faithless man
that he and all thy earth-bound ones
were doomed to die?

And when the great flood came upon earth
and all but two of all things breathing
the breath of life on dry land
and all the wingèd ones in air,
together with man—except for Noah
and those in the Ark—O Lord, didst thou
relent and spare thy first creations,
the innocent denizens of the deep?
Then were they lonely and dismayed
by the fate of their landed counterparts?

But when the wind of God thy spirit
swept over the earth again returning
dry land to man and beast. And the oceans
retreated with all their living ones
breathing not air but water.

And the Lord placed His bow in the sky
and He, and the heavens, wept no more,
as man, repentant, smiled to see
all creatures return to their earthly plane.
And whale and dolphin fishes and seal
octopus, turtle, shark, and eel
rejoiced, and reveled, and revel still
in their watery kingdom and domain.

OCEANS

OCEANS

They swell and subside, recede and rise,
the oceans of the world,
giving only glimpses to tantalize.
The mysteries of life they reveal and conceal.

Sea creatures swim, seabirds skim, but what lies
under those slapping sprays and stinging-tingling mists,
beneath those undulating sways, those watery graves?

Cold...cold...those blue-green/gray-blue waves,
dark, dark their sounding deeps, silent and profound
their secrets keeping. Far as the eye can see
curves and troughs and billows roll,
rising, falling, gathering strength as inevitably
as man's act, and art, of love.

From their hidden basined core
tsunami, tidal wave, typhoon race
earth-quaking seas to shore,
their driving, probing, surging surf
giving and, ever, taking away.

Ah, but they can be kind—
tender as lovers, brushing against continents,
caressing shores, embracing island lagoons,
flinging kisses heavenward !
In their streams'/currents' warm-cold flow
seals and dolphins gambol and play,
whales breach and sing and mate,
claspers clasped. Exulting
in the natural order of things.

(continuing)

(begin stanza 6)

Are they so different from you and me?
Those oceans/lovers of the sea?
Are not we, too, subservient
to acts of nature and man,
subject to sun and star,
seduced by the moon?
In our constant human quest
to co-exist with God's creation
of earth, sky, and sea.
Reveling in our place in His schemes,
delving, aspiring, giving birth
to our dreams.

LOVE DUET (the Gulf of Mexico and the Atlantic Ocean)

"Ho tante cose che ti voglio dire—o una sola, ma grande come il mare..." *

—Mimi to Rodolfo, *La Bohème* (Act IV)
(by Giacomo Puccini)

O tranquil tropic southern sea shall I
compare you to some holy Latin chant
some sacred music lapping at the soul?
Or some divine Puccini aria—Mimi's
or Cio-Cio-San's sublimely-rhymed
warm and tender plea of undying love?

And you O mighty ocean to the east
whose wind and wave fling boldly to and fro
upon your storm-borne lyre do you not play
such epic Wagner music-drama odes
as Isolde, singing *Liebestod,*
and Loge's ringing *Magic Fire* ?

Oh where but in your infinite symphony of seas
can we better hear the music of the spheres!

IN REMEMBRANCE OF SIDNEY LANIER

Long you have shone, Lanier
shining still warmly upon us
as the sun's infinite radiance
illumines our longing for truth.
Your voice
in its music
lingers
past the woods
through the glades
beyond death;
a song of things known
and unknown.
And the soft coastal winds
in the marsh
fill the poet
as the poem
with life's breath.

Consumed in your passion to live
evangel of lyric, of love
to speak of the ultimate dream
not to die with the dream unuttered
transcending your burning struggle
you reconcile nature with God.

(continuing)

(begin stanza 3)

Bright scholar
brief beacon of light
your poetry speaks to us all
that *feeling*
is all to the artist
and still can be all to man.
Your spirit your words
are mirrored
not in sand not even upon
your beloved mysterious islands
your mystical marshes of Glynn
but tenderly bravely
undying
in the minds
and hearts
of men.

CRESCENDO (Tybee Island)

But yesterday the sea was calm, serene,
a smooth unruffled bed on which to lie;
a woman, awaiting her lover. When he arrives
they embrace, tender, full of love—though it hides
quiet beneath the surface, just inside.
Then, it washes over them in gathering waves
yet to be revealed; and he is gentle still.

Today, in but a moment, so it seems,
all is changed. Rough the waters crash, loudly
on the shore, eager in lovemaking to the earth.
Sky and sea are gray; cloud-veiled the sun
from the secret mysteries of the deep. The lovers kiss,
anointing one another with their love.
And their ocean claims dominion over all.

BARRIER ISLANDS — Tybee and Little Tybee, Georgia

It is hot and still on these island waterways. Our boat,
a small canopy-shaded skiff, piloted across open water
by our colorful native-Savannah guide, now idles along
the narrow *allées* of Little Tybee Isle—too shallow
even at high tide for speed. The salt-marsh grasses,
sturdy, serene in their cool, murky, nutrient-rich waters,
grow lush and green on either side of us. In the distance
wide hammocks of trees stand guard, oak and palm and pine,
mysterious, dark, sharp contrast to these bright-sworded
blades saluting our passing wake. Byways
temptingly beckon, but only someone all-knowing
can choose the right path. Which turn shall we take?
Some unwary venturers, bird-watchers mostly,
become distracted, disoriented and lose their way.
Lost, trapped amid reaches of wetland earth, do they
encounter indwelling spirits of the Island's first inhabitants—
those early Indian tribes, Crete, Yamaha, Sioux—and implore
safe passage through their preeminent domain?

Sun-lit quiet unbroken but by lapping swells
calms our city-brought/over-wrought sensibilities.
We slow to a stop at a sea-swept stretch of sand and wade ashore
to gather shells—abundant along these hard-packed strands—
once housing living creatures, pale remnants now recalling
the ocean's returning might, its looming presence reigning,
its gathering force enduring just beyond our sight.
The somnolent sound of far-off surf, pale blue over blue
sky above sea, soothing, spell-binding, moves us to poetic song.

A family of brown pelicans lazily drowse and observe.
Later they'll arrow north for the night. White egrets dive
for their lunch, and great blue herons grant us space.
Other resident wildlife hide, awaiting the moon's *carte blanche* to hunt.
But then, back by the docks, we meet sleek dolphins nosing about
returning shrimpers' hulls, smiling, teasing for a treat. They pose
for our eager photos but, unrewarded, fall back—yet attuned,
communing between our two worlds in their own benevolent way.

(continuing)

Too soon our island idyll ends and we must disembark.
Still, Tybee Isle awaits—its promise of waves endlessly breaking,
pounding on shore, revealing only a trace of the ocean's mystic bond
with our humanity, whether near, upon, or within its deeps,
concealed but plain to prescient souls reveling in the light.
The contrast is extreme between Tybee and Little Tybee—
the one vacation pilgrims' mecca, the other larger but remote
whose silence and solitude recharge us, body and mind,
gracing us with the shades of those who lived, and loved, before.

Claim to these barrier islands, these secret waterways, is theirs—
this ancient allure, hidden, profound, this Mystery of the Lord's
"gathering together of waters and land"—primeval, pristine, and pure.
Revisiting them for a while strengthens us in our resolve to return.
But now we must go back to all that passes for modern civilization,
to our own Divinely-guided fates: cosmic, eternal, unknown.

THE TIDES (Tybee Isle)

Last night the sea boldly cast upon
the bosom of the shore, the rising tide
asserting its mastery of the land.
And we, exulting in beginning our new Day,
entwine as lovers will, by daylight
and by night, and give no thought to tomorrow.

Soon enough this happy time will end
and we will watch the tides start to withdraw,
far out to sea. But we do not weep
to see them go, these waves, these Days,
for they, and we, happily shall return.
The ocean—like our love—is deep, and eternal.

POINT OF VIEW

The death of the Earth will be beautiful,
surpassing its birth, the physicists say,
Breathtaking, vast (for so little belief)
clouds/fire profaning the air, raining tears
from the eyes of a thousand suns, Earth quakes;
tornadoes, hurricanes, whirl into one;
even oceans burn—colors churn, white-hot.
Never mind that the dead cannot see. And
besides, from what hiding place can we stare?
Jupiter? Venus? Mars? Farthest away
is best. Too near, a gray impenitence,
a too Vesuvian ash may obscure
Hiroshima/Nagasake/the world,
and an unearthly, far lovelier, Light.

TSUNAMI

An Elegy for Southeast Asia—26 December 2004.

Now shall we tell our inmost thoughts—of that profound
moment of truth, between breath and death? We, too, with you,
are borne on that cresting wave, that wall of wild sea water breaking
away from Earth's great core: that quaking mating-marriage bed
of thrusting plate and yielding crust, spawning cosmic birth.
Yet who can think and speak, rejoice and weep like Deity,
in such divinely-rhymed superlatives of anguish and of joy!
Although, God knows, we've seen His Magnitude, His sovereignty, before.
But has Earth itself ever thus trembled on its course, its plane,
its axis, fixed, ordained—and long held to be—steadfast?
Once death and I nearly met on fate's threshold of near-drowning,
in a mere three feet of careless seas—undertow, I suppose,
on such a bright and carefree day. On familiar Southern shores
edging the Atlantic. Upended, swallowing from that shallow brink
of an ocean fathomless, panicked burning throat and eyes cannot tell
if air still somehow waits—or if salvation, somewhere, dwells.
Although soon set aright by a savior, a samaritan nearby.
Did you reach out in mute appeal for fragile human touch,
floating on tides of hope and dread, those rising falling ocean swells?
As brother, sister, parent or mate, husband, wife, lover or child
held fast to your saving grasp—or cried out "Farewell!" Thousands
perished so, and yet the wonder is the miracle that graces souls
to survive, and rise, whether the body lives or dies.
It's said some primal urge and scheme, some inner sense God-given
from Creation's time, enables animals to circumvent upheaval
by such planetary tolls, earthquake or tidal wave, and seek
the hills above, that place where safety lies. So might we,
in all our sudden unforeseen earthly agonies of shock and aftershock,
embrace alike our days of utter joy, our nights of bitter grief, keeping fixed
our gaze, our thoughts and dreams, our hopes and fears, on higher ground.

AT SEA (in the Indian Ocean)

Today the ocean is smooth, gleaming
like blue-gray slate or marble and I,
alone on deck, stare in awe. Horizon
so wide too calm to imagine
such beauty marred, the tranquility,
the silent wonder of all I survey.

Oh might a pod of whales slice through
the skin of the sea and slap their flukes
smartly on high to catch my eye? Or
a circus of dolphins just to please me
dive and leap, arching their backs
as if to say, "Catch us, man,
if you can!" Others have seen but I,
loving them sight unseen, wait, and
standing my lone watch search in vain—
though yesterday squads of flying fish
launched by our wake and a banded snake
showed themselves to me.

Capricious though she may be, arrayed
in her many colors—seafoam, cobalt, indigo,
turquoise, her many moods—wild and free,
I never shall lose my beguiled fascination
with the vagaries of the sea. I'm content
with the few of her varied wonders
she deigns to reveal to me.

SAVANNAH SUNRISE

on Tybee Beach

Obscured by clouds, the sun waits for its cue
to break through night's enchanted dark
and assume the luminance of day.

The salty tide bids the shore *adieu.*
Fine sands blow rhythmically this way and that
while sea gulls await the coming warmth—
cold sentinels, above the gray-blue ocean's
foaming water line.

The clouds draw back, parting
like an ancient Sea ordained
by a mighty hand to let the Exiles pass,
that hidden mysteries
of the firmament and deep,
may, like the face of Deity
that His appointed heralds keep,
be, in part, revealed.

Finally the sun bursts forth
on peaceful skies and throbbing seas,
gilding still-wind-driven dunes and waves,
shining brighter light on our perceptions,
our human artist's-eye for *chiaroscuro*—
as in Earth's constant, natural, measured change
that is the heart and soul of things.
Of birth and breath and death and life,
of darkness into light,
of love into *Love*
and poetry into art.

REFLECTIONS, On The Island of St. George

As artist-poet, Michelangelo
first saw Creation's images meet
(as the novelist/cinema makers claim)
upon the horizon's wide-high sweep
where marble mountains reaching meet
the clouds over Settignano, so
this poet's questing vision keeps
watch on the St. George sea.

Over the blue-green deeps there drift
bands of hue-streaked clouds reflecting
the wayward moods of ocean and sky:
now luminous, light, now leaden and gray.
Backdrop for flights of pelicans, gulls
skimming the waves that ripple and glide
glitter and shimmer, darken then shine,
enticing dolphins to leap and dive.

Pure, pristine, the island lies
shell-strewn beaches deserted, remote
white sands renewing ancient ties
to a timeless rhyme, tempest and tide.
And these few words from Shakespeare's pen
echo our common language and art
as the King exhorts his men to *"Cry—
God for Harry! England and Saint George!"*

LATE ENTRY

In my mind I'm embarked on an uncharted star-lit sea—
a poet, seeking the ultimate prize this late summer's eve.
My body, too, seems eager to sail beyond the waiting dark,
giving still living breath to *words*, impassioned ever to believe
this deathless art of Poetry will long out-live my fragile barque.

Unlike the mind's emotions my feet and limbs keep losing feeling,
except for pain. Bone scrapes on bone, muscle and sinew contract
in spasms agonizing—reminders not unwelcoming crying *I am still here!*
Prescriptions multiply to a laughable degree, each new trial outwitted by
organisms colonizing, invisible to the naked eye.

My once pleasant aspect gone, yet I cannot shrink
from the images I portray. It's not complete, this task
driving art and me: I still can write a poem, can still
collect them for a book. What more can a poet ask?

(continuing)

(begin stanza 4)

Echoing Michelangelo's octogenarian lament:
"Crickets chirp in both my ears…" , so mine
disorient…and voice and vision pale and dim….
Yet we sail on, my faithful craft and I!—borrowing
brilliant burning stars from Earth's far canopy of space
to set in place like rare and priceless jewels, precious stones,
on my would-be-immortal page, not outweighed
even by thought and memory of my childhood passion
to create, happily foretelling my fourscore and ten.

I would not dare bargain with a much too gracious God,
nor wish to re-navigate my vanished youth. Becalmed, I am replete.
Late years gladly spent prove life is sweet when there's still time
for body and mind, soul and heart to live and laugh and love again,
awaiting that Divinely written, yet to be read, poetic ending rhyme.

MIDNIGHT MOONLIGHT

Remembering Tybee...

The moon shines still upon thee and me
though now we lie far, far apart.
It sails the night sky like a sailor the sea,
island to island, heart to heart.
Would that we could make ports of call,
revisiting all, one by one, on sight,
but we've set our sails to reach landfall
between evening star and the sun's shining light.

FIRST ANNIVERSARY, at Tybee Beach

A silvered light the morning sun breaks
over these rolling, swelling seas
reclaiming their right to the shifting dunes
on this our bright southeastern isle.
A mirrored refraction, glittering, gleaming,
its shimmering path like the moon's golden streaming,
its gentle heaving/breathing sights...rising, falling—
like the breath of lovers, beached, at ease.

Later the wintry sky may cast
a different, subdued, less stylish view.
Tide receding/afternoon-into-evening
darkling clouds suddenly lowering
their steely grayness over waves remaining
the same, ever-changing, a constant renewing:
surging, ebbing, surging again—
like playful love, on human shores.

Only last year almost to the day
our ocean lay waiting, our life beginning,
brimming with mysteries, seen, unseen.
Flights of seabirds eagerly skimming
over cool dark shapes dimly imagined
under blue-green waters plankton-rich,
schooled in promises—years unrolling
like breakers before us, one by one.

Diamonds are hard, hardly to be broken, but if they could
would they not cascade, brilliant as light, soft as rain
or waterfall, into Earth's wide and deep, bittersweet,
tilting/tempting wine bowls, filling to overflowing
all our perilous and intoxicating oceans and seas?
So they seem to me, these constant rolling waves, diamond bright,
and hard, forever thundering, breaking asunder before me.

And would not sapphires—real, not man-made—
those ocean-toned stones, pulverized on some exotic shore,
pour over Venus, rising from the sea
and make for her a crown, a diadem of azure blue?
So they appear, these lustrous blues
of canopied skies and luminous seas, to me.

And emeralds—how mystifying that they
might liquefy and spill all their blue-green secrets
into one divine opulence of colors—aqua, sea-foam green,
gold and cerulean blue: a gilded merging ocean/river-bed
where Rhinemaids sing and play in spirited array.
I see them in the swirling depths off Tybee's timeless pier!

And rubies never redder, from ever-burning sun year by year,
stream overhead in morning and in evening light
over shifting sands and guiding tides, sunrise and sunset.

But pearls. Ah, *pearls* ! Translucent alabaster's soul-like pure
perfection, anointing darkening seas with their unearthly beauty of moon-
drenched night. All these I see, and more, till I am moved to drink to
Neptune's water-gods for showering upon me all their deep-filled treasure-
cache of jewel-prism'd hues, on these my impassioned, romantic island
views of oceans and of seas.

AU CLAIR DE LA LUNE

You see me in the blue distances where ocean,
sky and mountain meet, mingling their loveliness
on a foreign shore,
a far-off horizon.
Am I a ship, waiting to set sail
to you, my enchanted island mooring?
Or Venus, drawing you to me *au clair
de la lune*, into my shell, my spell?
Near or far the sea's mirror shimmers,
lighting our way to one another,
beyond all the ways Time can betray us.

I hear, my Circean one, your lyric cries:
you are Dante dreaming of Beatrice,
Petrarca pining for your Laura,
Francis, lauding earth and heaven.
I feel your glance, your breath, upon me
like the sculptor's eye that sees
his marble figure in beauty hidden
before he gives it to the world.
Like the composer's silent ear, hearing,
still, the music he will write.

All I've desired you have given me.
This gift I give you...myself, to keep,
as I wrap myself in your visions of light,
beribbon myself by the light of the moon
as we come to our fated trysting place...
for you, my love, in our timeless sea.

ABOUT THE AUTHOR

Patricia Anne Kirby Craddock was born in Atlanta, Georgia. Graduate of The Academy of St. Genevieve-of-the-Pines in Asheville, North Carolina, she attended Georgia State College for Women (Milledgeville) and Oglethorpe University. A founding member of the Georgia State Poetry Society, she is a member of the Poetry Society of America and the Academy of American Poets. In 1982, she was elected a Life Fellow of the International Academy of Poets, Cambridge, England.

www.ingramcontent.com/pod-product-compliance
Lightning Source LLC
Chambersburg PA
CBHW022123280326
41933CB00007B/516